How to Nurture Your Spiritual Life

The Five Steps to Achieving Spiritual Freedom

Published by Lorena Evans

Copyright 2016 I Speak Spirit™

Lorena Evans

www.ispeakspirit.com

Follow us on [Facebook]{.underline} at:

www.facebook.com/ispeakspirit

and [Instagram]{.underline} at:

www.instagram.com/ispeakspirit/

and [Twitter]{.underline} at:

www.twitter.com/ispeakspirit/

BONUS! Book your Complementary Breakthrough Session Now!

https://calendly.com/ispeakspirit/30min

Download the **FREE** Exercise Workbook to accompany this book at:

http://ispeakspirit.net/workbook

Contents

DEDICATION

This book is dedicated to:

1) My smart and ready-to-take-charge readers out there.

2) My family who made me learn a second language which helped me write this book.

3) My Boo Boo who pushed me to stop Facebooking and finish my book.

ACKNOWLEDGMENTS

I want to thank my mom who let me read her metaphysical books at a very early age and my dad who taught me to work hard and be responsible. My "Nitas" (sisters) who helped build my character by giving me a hard time. My tutors Brenda Ridgeway, Lorraine Meyer, Gabrielle Orr, Ellena Lieberman and all of the great tutors from SNUI, a Branch of The Spiritualists' National Union, especially Margaret Challenger and Cathy Leigh Tsoukalas. Thanks to the Arthur Findlay College, England, and De Zwanenhof, Holland, for allowing me the opportunity to study there. My aunt, uncles, cousins, neighbors and friends that believe in me and my vision. To Karla, for the good times and inspiration, you are deeply missed. Last, but not least, to the love of my life, because you've taught me not to count the years but to make the years count.

INTRODUCTION - ABOUT ME

My name is Lorena. Since you're reading this, you may be wondering why I call my company I **Speak Spirit™.** Speaking "Spirit" is a unique language that I learned the same way we all learn our native language. In my case, "Spirit" is like a second language. I learned to speak spirit by blending my energy with energy in another realm. In the same way that some people translate other languages, I translate spirit. This is why **I Speak Spirit™**

When I was very young, I saw beings that had crossed over. I was too young to understand what I was seeing (that would come later!). I thought that everyone could see and communicate with the beings. At that young age, I did not realize that I was a spiritual medium. To me, seeing and speaking with spirits was as normal as brushing my teeth in the morning.

Despite being comfortable with my abilities now, the funny thing is, when it first happened as a child, I was scared to communicate with them! It can be a very scary process when you are too young to fully understand what's going on. I would wake up in the middle of the night and see a spirit standing in my doorway or next to my bed - a spirit that needed help. Seeing an uninvited guest in your room is not what you expect to wake up to! Eventually, I learned that these visits weren't anything to be scared of, but it took a while for me to be comfortable with my gifts and abilities. To tell you the truth, I still don't like to wake up and see someone in my room! (Privacy please!)

> Fun Fact: I used to play the piano and had a group with school friends called *The New Girls Sensation.*

When I was twelve, I read all of my mother's metaphysical books about love and the power of attraction. The information and purpose behind the power of positive attraction really resonated with me. I began to practice the methods and ideas taught in these books. At first, I began to practice my newly acquired power as an experiment. I just wanted to see if it worked or not.

Soon, I began finding things I had lost and I could wish for things that would come into my life. The more I practiced, the more I was able to harness this power of manifesting good by putting good out in the world. The possibilities and results were almost endless. Once in a while I would wonder why it would not work consistently.

After many years of trial and error, I was finally able to figure it out. One of the many formulas I learned and understood was that desire alone was not sufficient.

If we combine the intention with the right emotion we have one of the formulas for success! The power of attraction is such an amazing and exciting topic that I could write a book on the topic. With the right formula, you can make the power of attraction your personal assistant!

Want to share your story with me? Book your Complementary 30-Minute Intuitive Coaching Consultation and Let's Talk about It!

https://calendly.com/ispeakspirit/30min

Even if you are not familiar with the law of attraction, it can help you. Think of it like this: You may not understand how gravity works, but if you drop something, I promise you it will hit the ground. The law of attraction works the same way. The Universe and the law of attraction really want you to receive what you want in life.

They're waiting for you to turn on the light switch so your light can shine. I feel that I was born to spread this knowledge and wisdom to others. Even when I was first reading about the laws of positive attraction in my mother's books, it felt familiar to me - like I'd learned it before. Whether I was accessing past life information or the familiar, the Universe was happy.

I finally woke up to one of the universal truths around me. I'm happy to share this with you in an effort to help you manifest your greatest hopes. I want you to be happy and--more importantly--the Universe wants you to be happy, too.

> Fun Fact: I created a plan to build a rocket to communicate with my alien friends. *We forgot the part about making it fly, so it never worked.*

During high school and college, I let my spiritual gifts go dormant. I got caught up in the fast-paced lifestyle of school and everything that goes with it. It's funny how it always seems to work that way. Our innate abilities go dormant and wake up when we need them most.

My re-connection came years later when I was in my early thirties. My sense of spiritual purpose hit me like a truck and I knew what I wanted to do. More importantly, I knew what I needed to do. I needed to help others learn to use and trust their own internal tools and resources. Suddenly, I was on a mission that was leading me down a new but still familiar path.

My internal sources were asking me the right questions and the Universe began to open avenues for me to receive the correct answers.

In a way, I felt like a passenger on a train that had no brakes and no clue as to whether the train would stop. It was up to me and only me to take advantage of this sudden wealth of information that was coming my way from Spirit. I knew I needed to open myself up to these new opportunities coming my way and learn as much as I could.

Fun Fact: I'm a self-taught golfer who as a child became the National Golf Champion in the Dominican Republic winning more than 80 tournaments nationwide.

On Friday, February 21, 2014, I received a call from my dad close to midnight. I remember waking up and getting a bit nervous as he never calls so late at night. I did not pick up at first and chose to text him back as I was not ready to hear anything that he might have to say. When I read his message, I suddenly understood why; he told me that my cousin Karla had passed in a car accident.

Growing up, Karla and I were very close and as adults we spent as much time together as possible. She was more like a sister than a cousin. Even though I had several losses in my family in the past, Karla's death really hit close to home. I knew there was another life and another side where we do not die - we just cross over.

I was desperate to communicate with her one last time and I made it my personal mission to find a way to do so. I found a conference on mediumship near my home, and once again, the path was opened wide for me. Once I set my mind to something, I do not stop till I achieve it. You can do the same by reading and accepting what resonates in your heart, challenging your own mind and questioning every conviction that has been programmed into you. Sometimes, what we are told as *truth* is someone else's *truth*.

One of my greatest accomplishments in developing my psychic and mediumistic abilities has been studying at the Arthur Findlay College in England. I had to prepare for this though. I joined an amazing group of people and we would meet on a weekly basis to practice and do what is called in mediumship "sitting in the power." This is a technique used for the connection and development of psychic and mediumistic abilities.

I continued my studies and became a Reiki Master, Akashic Records Consultant, Angel Card Reader and Teacher, developing medium and a Certified Professional Life Coach; combined all of these tools into one: **Intuitive Coach and Spiritual Strategist**! Bam! How do you like that!

THE FIVE STEPS (SECRETS) TO SPIRITUAL FREEDOM: NEMO

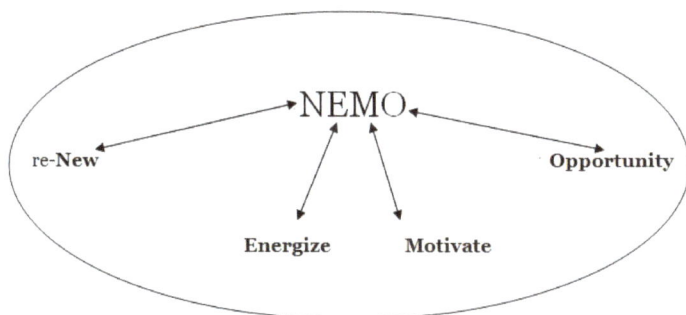

FIGURE: WHAT NEMO MEANS

You're probably wondering exactly what NEMO stands for. I get that question a lot. I even joke that after ninety days you'll "find your NEMO." (Don't sue me Disney. LOL) The idea of NEMO is all about shifting your reality with techniques that will re-**New** your Perspective, **Energize** your soul, **Motivate** your spirit, and open any doors to the new **Opportunities** in your life. Not bad for a month and a half of your time.

Just think of the lifetime of benefits. When you learn to recognize and accept what makes you unique, you'll learn how to use this talent for self-development. You are the only one that can truly make your life better.

I can guide you, but you manifest the results. NEMO helps you focus on becoming the new you-- the *you* you were meant to be--all while connecting with great resources to help you on your path.

The five steps to spiritual freedom are meant to help you develop your soul's guidance system and activate your soul's Global Positioning System (GPS) to help bring you closer to your life's purpose. Taking these steps will allow you to learn what your path is and help you achieve your goals and the good fortune you deserve.

Taking these first steps may help bring you closer to your path of clarity and joy. Don't worry about doing this alone. I will be here to guide you through each and every step. I'm always happy to help. Let's begin.

Do you feel like you're at a crossroads in life or like you're stuck in a ditch not able to figure out where to go or what to do next? Do you feel like you know a direction that you want to go but have no idea how to get moving? Have you been reading spiritual and metaphysical books but still find yourself lost and confused? Do you feel stuck? If you answered *yes* to any of these questions, don't worry.

You're not alone and it's definitely not your fault that you're feeling like this. It's very easy to find yourself feeling lost without proper guidance. That's where I can help. I'll help you discover what you want out of life, switch this new information over to the spiritual side, and then I will give you the tools to find your answers. Only you can make the choices, but I'll be here to help you find the way and to provide the support you need. The tools you need are all in these secrets, but--more importantly--the tools are inside you. You just need to learn how to access them.

Before we dive in to the five secrets, it is important for you to be aware of where you stand at this exact moment. This is the only way you will be able to experience and acknowledge the shift and truly enjoy the transformation. Now, let's put some thought on each category mentioned below. Rate it from 1-10. (1) means you are not very happy in this category right now and (10) means you are very happy in this aspect of your life.

1.	Spirituality	1	2	3	4	5	6	7	8	9	10
2.	Relationships	1	2	3	4	5	6	7	8	9	10
3.	Health	1	2	3	4	5	6	7	8	9	10
4.	Money	1	2	3	4	5	6	7	8	9	10
5.	Self	1	2	3	4	5	6	7	8	9	10

If you are 100% satisfied with your life now and you got all 10's, good for you! Drop the Book slowly and continue doing whatever you are doing! If you are not 100% satisfied, please take time to explain WHY you score less than a 10 using the spaces below.

Spirituality

....
....
....
....

Relationships

....
....
....
....

Health

....
....
....
....

Money

....
....
....
....

Self

....
....
....
....
....

Is your picture a bit clearer now? Don't be sad or mad if you are a bit disappointed with your starting point. The reality is that the more you need to accomplish to get to your happy place, the more impactful your transformation will be! This is already a great achievement - the fact that you have clarity about where you are. I will guide you through the process and help you get to where you want to be. Let's do it!

Secret #1 - New Perspective

The word **New** is charged energetically and vibrationally with great positive energy. It represents beginnings, creation, rebirth and all of the words and feelings that bring about a sense of hope and light at the end of the tunnel. It's the natural first step on your journey of discovery.

Re-**N**ewing your perspective starts with taking responsibility for your thoughts and perceptions. You need to acknowledge that all that surrounds us is our own creation. Do you like the experience that you are living? Great! Don't change anything. If you do not like it, you must make the conscious decision to change your perspective of the reality you are living.

Coming from a Third World country, my perception of what my life was supposed to be was very different than what it is now. I recall having limiting beliefs that I couldn't achieve more than the little I had. I perceived that nothing more was possible, so no changes were able to take place.

This situation changed when, at a very young age, my parents started sending me on summer vacations out of the country. To my surprise, I perceived reality beyond what I thought was possible. I let go of my limiting beliefs once I discovered there was a bigger and better world out there that I could be a part of. I became who I am today because I allowed myself to renew my perspective.

What if you can't become a world traveler and see what's out there beyond your home? Don't worry. You can still renew your perspective by nurturing the ever evolving world of opportunities that come your way. When you nurture these opportunities, you allow a new perception to be born.

Understanding the ever-evolving world helps you to be open, to accept and flow with change. No matter who we are and what we have in life, we all have the power of choice. When we utilize this power, we become free. In practical terms, here are some tips on how to achieve a NEW perspective in life:

1. Remember that we are spiritual beings living a human experience. Don't take life so seriously!

2. Love and accept yourself exactly as you are. *You are Perfect.*

3. Don't judge yourself and beat yourself up for your past experiences. Good or bad, those experiences made you who you are today!

4. Write a list of the characteristics of your "current world." Next to it, write a list of the characteristics of your "ideal world." Notice the difference and commit to one action for the next week. Every week select a new action and get closer to your ideal world!

5. Write a list of characteristics that you admire in people that you know. If you can perceive it, you can be it! We only notice and attract to our lives what is in our same vibration, so own it and start acting on these characteristics because you have them already!

What are the ten things in your life that you take WAY too seriously? It can be anything!

1. ....
2. ....
3. ....
4. ....
5. ....
6. ....
7. ....
8. ....
9. ....
10. ....

For all of these things, ask yourself the following:

1. Is it life threatening?
2. Is it health threatening?
3. Is it endangering me or anyone else?
4. Is it life changing?

If the answer is *no* to at least 50% of these questions, you must let go of that thing! Changing it is NOT that SERIOUS!

Every time you catch yourself getting intense or too serious regarding something, ask yourself these questions and evaluate if change is worth it!

Secret #2 - ENERGIZE Your Soul

I love talking about energizing our souls. We are so busy doing so much in life that we forget to stop, take a breath, and take care of ourselves. We end up depleted in all aspects of our lives. Living the American dream, I realized that I was not getting enough "time to dream."

On top of that, I had very little time to rest or time to appreciate the accomplishments I already achieved. When our energy levels drop and we don't have energy stored up from resting and appreciating what we have achieved, we start to feel sick, confused and bitter, and we start making mistakes in all aspects of life. If you are running this trail, *you are not alone.* This is one of the biggest challenges we face in modern society when trying to achieve spiritual freedom. How can we achieve freedom when we are trapped in our own expectations, societies' expectations, and everyone else's expectations?

The truth is that no one's opinion or expectations should matter. Not even yours! We feed our bodies nutrients to keep healthy and to survive. We also need to nourish the soul in the same manner.

To help you achieve optimal soul nourishment and energy, here are some tips you can incorporate in your daily life:

Experience life as an observer and without judgment.

Nature is your friend - visit it more often.

Exercise regularly. Your body is the vessel of your soul and needs to be taken care of.

Rejuvenate your soul with alone time, journaling, and meditation.

Ground yourself with words and thoughts of gratitude.

Innovate your thoughts by utilizing reinforcing affirmations. Change your thoughts; change your world.

Zoom out of every situation and try to see the bigger picture. You might find the path less traveled and enjoy the journey with less effort. The more possibilities we see in a certain scenario, the easier it is to make the right choice.

Enjoy what you have and forget about what you wish for. It is only from a place of fullness that we can achieve more.

Resting, sleeping and eating right play a huge part in our lives, but without nurturing our souls with the fuel that keeps us moving toward life's purpose and striving for expansion and greatness, there isn't much to sustain us when life gets difficult.

If you don't stop to energize your soul, you end up feeling like a failure. If you adopt these tips to E.N.E.R.G.I.Z.E. your soul, in only a couple of days, you will feel a great shift inside and outside your world!

Bonus Exercise: What are your favorite activities?

Write a list of activities that you enjoy. It can be anything. What activities make you happy and make your heart jump when you do them?

1. ....
2. ....
3. ....
4. ....
5. ....
6. ....
7. ....
8. ....
9. ....
10. ....

What do you notice from this list? Are these activities expensive to do? Or free? What is stopping you today from doing them?

GOAL: Select at least one activity that you will commit to doing this week. Every week select another one until it becomes a habit.

SECRET #3 - MOTIVATE YOUR SPIRIT

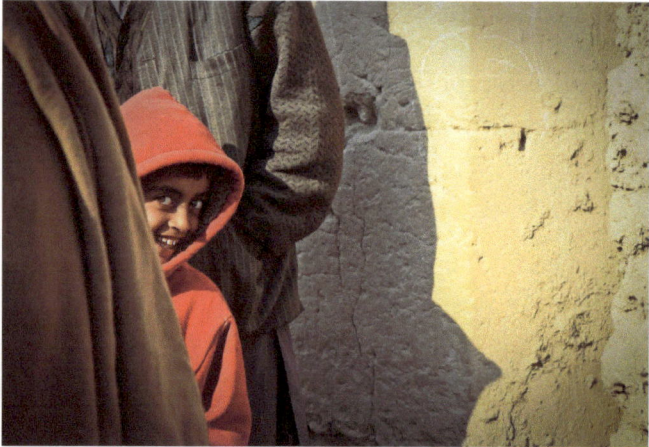

Just as it's hard to motivate yourself to do certain things like clean the house or get up early for work, it can be just as hard to motivate your spirit. We're used to giving ourselves pep talks to get through daily tasks, but how do we give our spirit a pep talk? You do it by setting a goal at the soul level and reminding yourself that it is your highest purpose.

Think about what will make you experience peace and harmony. Don't get distracted by the material things in life. Reach beyond that to what makes you feel whole on the soul level. When are you happiest? What were you doing that made you feel at peace? Pinpoint it. That is your highest purpose.

I work a regular 9-5 high-stress job. I like what I do, but I know that what really motivates me is helping others through my I Speak Spirit™ journey. Helping others is my highest and best purpose. That is what I was born to do. The goal that motivates me at the soul level is knowing that I'm fulfilling this commitment and that I'm preparing to devote all my time to my purpose.

It's a long-term goal, but I know how peaceful I feel when I'm able to help someone use my tools and life experiences. This sense of purpose helps keep me motivated and reaching for my goal - even on days when it seems far off. Everyone has a higher purpose. What is yours? Write it down. Commit to working toward it.

Here are some tips to keep your spirit motivated on the journey:

- **Act on your inspiration.** You get your best results when you use your best energy. Turn your ideas into action. If you find your motivation slipping, talk to someone about why your goal is so important to you. By voicing what we love about our soul's purpose, it's easier to find that inspiration all over again.

- **Ask questions that move you forward.** When faced with a roadblock on your spiritual journey, instead of giving up, ask questions. Questions help us problem solve, and soon you can overcome anything blocking your way. Ask yourself questions like "What's a better way?" or "How can I have fun doing this?" or "What experiences do I want to create?" or "How do I want to spend more time each day?"

- **Be your own motivational coach, not a critic.** It's true you are your own worst enemy. We can also be our best motivational coaches. When you find your motivation drooping, give yourself a pep talk! If you need support with this, I highly recommend interviewing a couple of Spiritual Coaches to see which one is a great fit for you!

- **Be the change you want to see.** Instead of trying to change everyone around you, change yourself and watch the ripple effect that follows. Lead by example.

- **See problems as challenges that can be overcome.** Instead of being bogged down by seemingly insurmountably problems, reframe your reference. They're not problems, they're challenges. Challenges are opportunities for growth, for achieving excellence, and for doing your personal best. Keep the motivation up and you will achieve your goals! We will discuss opportunities in depth when we discuss the next secret.

BONUS EXERCISE: LOVE YOUR REFLECTION

When was the last time you told yourself how awesome you are and how much you love yourself? We are very quick to judge and criticize our every move, but rarely do we take the time to acknowledge and enjoy the perfect beings that we are as the exact creation from source.

For this exercise, I encourage you to write a letter about why you love yourself exactly as you are. After doing so, read this letter aloud in front of a mirror. This exercise will help you recognize who you really are and help with building the rapport with yourself that you need. You are perfect, exactly as you are!

SECRET #4 - OPPORTUNITIES IN LIFE

The interesting thing about opportunities in life is that they present themselves just by the fact that we are alive. Sometimes these opportunities are small, single moments that are gone almost as quickly as they appear. It may seem that if we blink, we'll miss them. Other opportunities are clearly set in our spiritual path for a purpose. They're big and obvious and there's no way we could miss their significance!

Do not ignore opportunities for personal and spiritual growth when they enter your life. If we cannot see them, we cannot reach them, cannot understand them and cannot learn from them.

Coming from a Third World country where opportunities were not as prevalent as they are in the US, I developed a keen eye when it came to spotting opportunities. One of the things I did to shift my mindset to see more opportunities was to change my perception and my vocabulary.

For instance, I don't utilize the word *problem* or *issue*. Every time a situation comes about---good or bad--I always say, "Well this is an opportunity for _____ (fill in the blank)."

Of course it's not as easy as it sounds. We have to master the power of our thoughts, trust our intuition, and follow what we truly feel in our hearts.

When presented with an opportunity, it is important to face it or jump right into it. Sometimes when we think too much or overanalyze an opportunity, our fears and limiting beliefs block us from taking action. Remember to take action. Confronting each opportunity helps us on the road to spiritual growth.

Now, you may ask, "How do I know that what I have in front of me is a good opportunity?" I want you to focus on the fact that absolutely every situation we have in front of us is an opportunity. We should not judge. No matter what, there is always a message within.

Good or bad opportunities teach us to embrace and enhance our innate talents and spiritual gifts. The more you trust your intuition and divine guidance, the more you'll be able to understand your connection to the Universe. You'll be able to better understand the language of your heart and discern exactly what you need at certain moments.

In order for you to cultivate your intuition, you need to practice. You need to start jumping into the opportunities. Opportunities are ways to develop and nurture your spiritual growth.

Ten years ago, I was given the opportunity to move from the Dominican Republic to the United States. When I received the call telling me I got the job I applied for, I did not question it. I sold everything that I owned, and I didn't look back. I didn't stop to think if it was the right or wrong opportunity.

I noted that from this job opportunity other doors would open and amazing things could arise from just one choice. Don't focus so much on the specific opportunity being presented to you. Know that each opportunity is like a door to multiple opportunities and choices.

Passion is another important factor regarding opportunities in life. Passion is a great GPS when it comes to making the decision to follow a specific opportunity. Your passion will keep you going regardless of the situation or opportunity that is presented to you. Every opportunity is there to teach you a lesson. Your passion is going to keep you alive and going until the right opportunity comes your way.

Following are some things that can help you build momentum and jump into opportunities:

Open your perception and awareness to allow your soul to identify the opportunity.

Passion is the fuel that will keep you going regardless of the outcome.

Playfulness is the joy of living. Focus on the journey, not the destination.

Outcomes should never be the focus. The possibilities that the opportunity brings should be your focus.

Relax! There is no right or wrong! No matter which way you go, it is perfect for you.

Trust your gut feeling or intuition, as they are your soul's GPS. Intuition will take you to the right place at the right time.

Understanding the opportunity with your heart instead of your mind will help you see beyond what is in front of you.

Nurture your decision with positive affirmations.

Intention is a great tool to attract your dream opportunity.

Transform your mindset and vocabulary and eliminate the words *problem* or *issue*. Replace these negative words with *opportunity*.

You have the power to change your path. It is up to you to jump on the train to transformation!

CHOOSE FROM THESE POSSIBILITIES

Utilize the new way of seeing opportunities in life and the concept that there are no good or bad opportunities. Write ten opportunities that have been presented to you that you have not acted on. (Don't limit yourself to ten if you have more!)

1. ....
2. ....
3. ....
4. ....
5. ....
6. ....
7. ....
8. ....
9. ....
10. ....

Now, for each opportunity, ask yourself the following questions:

1. Why have I not jumped on this opportunity?
2. What is stopping me?
3. What will be the outcome if I take action now?
4. What other doors will this opportunity open for me?

Once you understand what is standing in your way, select one opportunity and run with it full force! Need someone to hold you accountable? Send me an email telling me what you'll do and now I WILL KNOW! @ lorena.evans@ispeakspirit.com

Secret #5 - Believe in yourself

"Believe in yourself" sounds so simple, but it can be one of the hardest secrets to learn. Sometimes it seems like we're almost programmed to NOT believe in ourselves. We overanalyze and second guess every little thing in our lives. That's no way to live and it's definitely no way to achieve your highest spiritual freedom.

In order to believe, you need to transform your mindset. Transforming your thoughts and, in turn, your actions plays an important role in the secrets. They combine in the final, biggest, secret - Believe. Here are some tips on how to believe in yourself and bring about positive changes in your life:

- **Move past your discomfort.** Discomfort is part of fear, which holds us back from reaching our ultimate goals and desires.

- **Be okay with people not agreeing with you.** Advice is all well and good, but you are the only one that knows what is written in your soul. You need to make your own decisions.

- **Trust yourself.** Self-doubt is normal, but if you trust yourself and your decisions, you can overcome self-doubt. Your path will become clearer.

- **Know that you are stronger than you think.** You can do anything. You can achieve your goals. Never doubt your strength. You are stronger than you know.

RID YOURSELF OF THE WORD IMPOSSIBLE

A great way to believe in yourself is to build up to it.
So, first I would like for you to gauge how much you
believe in yourself! No judgment, just think about it
and answer honestly. I will ask you the same
question at the end of this exercise.

Belief Level   1   2   3   4   5   6   7   8   9   10

Now, let's take a quick look at your past.

**Write down your five greatest
accomplishments.**

1. ....
2. ....
3. ....
4. ....
5. ....

Close your eyes now and think back and ask yourself?

1. Before achieving this accomplishment, did you think that you were going to be able to achieve it?
2. What gave you the strength or inspiration?
3. How did achieving this goal made you feel?
4. With one word, describe what achieving this goal gave you.

What characteristic or skills did you obtain from these achievements?

1.
2.
3.
4.
5.

Write down the people that supported you along the way.

1.
2.
3.
4.
5.

Close your eyes now and think back and ask yourself:

1. What words of encouragement were you given when you needed this support most?
2. What was their reaction when you achieved this goal?
3. How did having the support of these five people make you feel?

Ok, so now we have the **PROOF** of our past accomplishments and you have a **Skillset.** You achieved the accomplishments with the help of your **CHEERLEADING TEAM** which is your awesome support team! Ask yourself again, how much do I believe in myself?

Belief Level 1   2   3   4   5   6   7   8   9   10

Hurray! You got this! Now, next time you have self-doubt or feel insecure about your ability to achieve a goal or feel that you are all alone, look back at this list and remind yourself of your accomplishments! And if you could do it before, you can do it all over again!

CONCLUSION

I can't express how excited I am that you've decided to take the first steps on your journey to spiritual freedom. Take time to look around and really appreciate all that you see. The more you grow, the more aware you'll be concerning your own strength of purpose. If you need a friend on your path, remember that I'm here to cheer you on.

Believe in yourself; I already do.

Lorena Evans

I Speak Spirit™

http://ispeakspirit.com/

www.facebook.com/ispeakspirit

www.instagram.com/ispeakspirit

www.twitter.com/ispeakspirit